HUMMINGBIRD

By Rachel Rose

Minneapolis, Minnesota

Credits

Cover and title page, © Megan/Adobe Stock; 3, © Fireglo/Shutterstock; 4–5, © DGHayes/iStock; 6, © Chesampson/Adobe Stock, © Keneva Photography/Shutterstock; 7, © epantha/iStock; 9, © Satheesh Rajh Rajagopalan/iStock; 11, © Bird Images/iStock; 12–13, © phototrip.cz/Adobe Stock; 14–15, © Glass and Nature/Shutterstock; 17, © milehightraveler/iStock; 18–19, © Jim/Adobe Stock; 20, © betsy cooley/EyeEm/Adobe Stock; 21, © RobDemPhoto/Shutterstock; 22, © mr. Timmi/Shutterstock, © 1000s_pixels/Shutterstock; 23, © Ondrej Prosicky/Shutterstock.

Bearport Publishing Company Product Development Team
President: Jen Jenson; Director of Product Development: Spencer Brinker; Managing Editor: Allison Juda; Associate Editor: Naomi Reich; Senior Designer: Colin O'Dea; Associate Designer: Elena Klinkner; Associate Designer: Kayla Eggert; Product Development Specialist: Anita Stasson

Library of Congress Cataloging-in-Publication Data

Names: Rose, Rachel, 1968- author.
Title: Hummingbird / by Rachel Rose.
Description: Minneapolis, Minnesota : Bearport Publishing Company, [2024] | Series: Library of awesome animals | Includes bibliographical references and index.
Identifiers: LCCN 2023001671 (print) | LCCN 2023001672 (ebook) | ISBN 9798885099943 (hardcover) | ISBN 9798888221778 (paperback) | ISBN 9798888223093 (ebook)
Subjects: LCSH: Hummingbirds--Juvenile literature.
Classification: LCC QL696.A558 R67 2024 (print) | LCC QL696.A558 (ebook) | DDC 598.7/64--dc23/eng/20230223
LC record available at https://lccn.loc.gov/2023001671
LC ebook record available at https://lccn.loc.gov/2023001672

Copyright © 2024 Bearport Publishing Company. All rights reserved. No part of this publication may be reproduced in whole or in part, stored in any retrieval system, or transmitted in any form or by any means, electronic, mechanical, photocopying, recording, or otherwise, without written permission from the publisher.

For more information, write to Bearport Publishing, 5357 Penn Avenue South, Minneapolis, MN 55419.

Contents

Awesome Hummingbirds!.............. 4
Tiny Jewels 6
Up, Down, and All Around............ 8
Flower Power......................10
Quick Licks 12
Small Bird, Big Heart 14
Down South....................... 16
Showing Off...................... 18
Jelly Bean Babies 20

Information Station 22
Glossary 23
Index 24
Read More 24
Learn More Online 24
About the Author.................. 24

AWESOME Hummingbirds!

ZOOM! With its fast-beating wings, a hummingbird flits through the air. Small, speedy, and **agile**, hummingbirds are awesome!

THE HUMMINGBIRD GETS ITS NAME FROM THE SOUND ITS WINGS MAKE WHEN IT FLIES.

Tiny Jewels

There are many kinds of hummingbirds, but almost all of them are small. Most weigh less than a nickel!

In addition to being tiny, hummingbirds are very colorful. The feathers on their long wings are so bright, they are sometimes called flying **jewels**.

A rufous-crested coquette

An Anna's hummingbird

A bee hummingbird

THE BEE HUMMINGBIRD IS THE SMALLEST BIRD IN THE WORLD. MOST ARE ONLY 2 INCHES (5 CM) TALL.

Up, Down, and All Around

These small birds are great fliers. They can flap their wings between 20 and 200 times per second. **WOW!** And unlike most birds, hummingbirds can move their wings in every direction. The speed and movement of their wings allows them to **hover** in the air and fly backward.

Flower Power

Hummingbirds need a lot of **energy** to keep their bodies moving so quickly. They get it from the food they eat. Sometimes, they catch an insect midair for a quick buggy snack. But hummingbirds eat mostly sugary **nectar** from flowers. *YUM!* They need a lot of food, so they visit about 1,000 flowers every day.

> SCIENTISTS THINK HUMMINGBIRDS REMEMBER EVERY FLOWER THEY VISIT. THE BIRDS OFTEN GO TO THE SAME PLACES EVERY YEAR.

Quick Licks

How do hummingbirds get the nectar? They use their long, thin beaks to reach deep inside flowers. Then, they lap up the sweet liquid with tongues that are even longer.

A single lick doesn't pick up a lot—but that's not a problem. These speedy birds can take around 20 licks each second.

Small Bird, Big Heart

Hummingbirds need more than fast wings and lots of food to keep their small bodies going. They also need big, strong hearts. Their hearts pump at a rate of 1,200 beats per minute. That's nearly 10 times faster than a human's heart. **THUMP-THUMP, THUMP-THUMP!**

HUMMINGBIRDS HAVE THE LARGEST HEARTS COMPARED TO BODY SIZE OF ANY ANIMAL.

Down South

Hummingbirds live throughout North, Central, and South America. They can be found in many **habitats**, from tree-filled forests to rocky mountains.

When winter comes, North America gets cold. The birds that live there **migrate** south. Some travel as many as 500 miles (800 km) a day.

> HUMMINGBIRDS ARE **SOLITARY** BIRDS. WHEN THEY FLY SOUTH, THEY GO ALONE.

Showing Off

When spring approaches, it is time for migrating birds to return home. This is also when hummingbirds **mate**.

Each **male** works hard to get the attention of a **female**. He shows off his flying skills by diving and swooping around her. Once they've mated, it's time for the female to build a nest for her eggs.

MOTHER BIRDS USE LEAVES, FEATHERS, AND SOMETIMES SPIDERWEBS TO BUILD NESTS.

Jelly Bean Babies

Female hummingbirds usually lay two eggs at a time. Each is about the size of a jelly bean. After almost two weeks, the eggs hatch. Then, the mother feeds her chicks. At first, the babies eat mostly insects so they can grow quickly. After only a few weeks, the young birds are able to flit through the air in search of their own food.

Hummingbird eggs

A MOTHER HUMMINGBIRD CATCHES INSECTS AND CHEWS THEM UP BEFORE FEEDING THEM TO HER CHICKS.

Information Station

HUMMINGBIRDS ARE AWESOME!
LET'S LEARN EVEN MORE ABOUT THEM.

Kind of animal: Hummingbirds are birds. Like all birds, they are warm-blooded, are covered in feathers, and have wings.

More hummingbirds: There are more than 320 kinds of hummingbirds. One of the most common in the United States is the ruby-throated hummingbird.

Size: Most hummingbirds are about 4 in. (10 cm) long from beak to tail. That's about as long as a crayon!

HUMMINGBIRDS AROUND THE WORLD

WHERE HUMMINGBIRDS LIVE

Glossary

agile able to move around quickly and easily

energy the power used to move, grow, and live

female a hummingbird that can lay eggs to have baby birds

habitats places in nature where plants and animals usually live

hover to stay in one place in the air

jewels bright, colorful stones found in nature

male a hummingbird that can't lay eggs

mate to come together to have young

migrate to move from one place to another during a certain time of year

nectar a sweet liquid made by flowers

solitary alone

Index

beaks 12, 22
chicks 20–21
eggs 18, 20
female 18, 20
flowers 10, 12
habitats 16
hover 8
male 18
mate 18
migrate 16, 18
nectar 10, 12–13
tongues 12
wings 4–6, 8, 14, 22

Read More

Gray, Susan H. *Ruby-Throated Hummingbird Migration (Marvelous Migrations).* Ann Arbor, MI: Cherry Lake Publishing, 2021.

Riggs, Kate. *Hummingbirds (Amazing Animals).* Mankato, MN: The Creative Company, 2023.

Learn More Online

1. Go to **www.factsurfer.com** or scan the QR code below.
2. Enter "**Hummingbird**" into the search box.
3. Click on the cover of this book to see a list of websites.

About the Author

Rachel Rose writes books for kids and teaches yoga. She lives in California with her favorite animal—her dog, Sandy.